LIVE IT:
HONESTY

MOLLY ALOIAN

Crabtree Publishing Company

www.crabtreebooks.com

Author: Molly Aloian
Coordinating editor: Bonnie Dobkin
Publishing plan research and development:
   Sean Charlebois, Reagan Miller
   Crabtree Publishing Company
Editor: Reagan Miller
Proofreader: Crystal Sikkens
Editorial director: Kathy Middleton
Production coordinator: Margaret Salter
Prepress technician: Margaret Salter

Logo design: Samantha Crabtree
Project Manager: Santosh Vasudevan (Q2AMEDIA)
Art Direction: Rahul Dhiman (Q2AMEDIA)
Design: Neha Kaul and Parul Gambhir (Q2AMEDIA)
Illustrations: Q2AMEDIA
Front Cover: Philippe Quint thanks cab driver Mohammed Khalil
   for returning the priceless violin he left in his cab by mistake.
Title Page: Golfer Bobby Jones is congratulated for his honesty,
   even though it cost him an important championship.

Library and Archives Canada Cataloguing in Publication

Aloian, Molly
   Live it: honesty / Molly Aloian.

(Crabtree character sketches)
Includes index.
ISBN 978-0-7787-4881-6 (bound).--ISBN 978-0-7787-4914-1 (pbk.)

   1. Honesty--Juvenile literature. 2. Biography--Juvenile literature.
I. Title. II. Title: Honesty. III. Series: Crabtree character sketches

BJ1533.H7A46 2010   j179'.9   C2009-905370-5

Library of Congress Cataloging-in-Publication Data

Aloian, Molly.
   Live it-- honesty / Molly Aloian.
      p. cm. -- (Crabtree character sketches)
   Includes index.

   ISBN 978-0-7787-4914-1 (pbk. : alk. paper) -- ISBN 978-0-7787-4881-6
(reinforced library binding : alk. paper)
   1. Respect--Juvenile literature. 2. Biography--Juvenile literature. I.
Title.

BJ1533.H7A46 2010
179'.9--dc22
                                                          2009035500

Crabtree Publishing Company

www.crabtreebooks.com   1-800-387-7650

Printed in the USA/122009/BG20090930

Published in Canada
Crabtree Publishing
616 Welland Ave.
St. Catharines, ON
L2M 5V6

Published in the United States
Crabtree Publishing
PMB 59051
350 Fifth Avenue, 59th Floor
New York, New York 10118

Published in the United Kingdom
Crabtree Publishing
Maritime House
Basin Road North, Hove
BN41 1WR

Published in Australia
Crabtree Publishing
386 Mt. Alexander Rd.
Ascot Vale (Melbourne)
VIC 3032

CONTENTS

WHAT IS HONESTY?   4

HONESTY IN SPORTS   6

HONESTY VS. RICHES   10

BEING HONEST
WITH YOURSELF   14

HONESTY AND COURAGE   18

BEING HONEST
BECAUSE IT'S RIGHT   22

BEING HONEST
ABOUT MONEY   26

WEB SITES   30

GLOSSARY   31

INDEX   32

WHAT IS HONESTY?

HONESTY MEANS TELLING THE TRUTH NO MATTER WHAT. IF YOU'RE HONEST, YOU EARN OTHER PEOPLE'S TRUST AND THEIR RESPECT.

THERE ARE MANY DIFFERENT WAYS TO BE HONEST. YOU'LL LEARN ABOUT A FEW OF THOSE WAYS FROM THESE SIX AMAZING PEOPLE.

BOBBY JONES
PROFESSIONAL GOLFER

MOHAMMED KHALIL
CAB DRIVER

ELLEN SZITA
A 45-YEAR-OLD WHO COULDN'T READ

JEFFREY WIGAND
TOBACCO INDUSTRY INSIDER

KELLI OWENS
TRAINEE AT GOODWILL

ROBERT CUNNINGHAM
POLICE DETECTIVE

PHYLLIS PENZO
WAITRESS

BOBBY JONES

WHO IS HE?
A PROFESSIONAL GOLFER

WHY HIM?
HE WAS HONEST EVEN THOUGH IT COST HIM A CHAMPIONSHIP.

SOME ATHLETES WILL DO ANYTHING TO WIN, EVEN IF IT MEANS BEING DISHONEST. BUT NOT BOBBY JONES. IN FACT, HE ONCE PLAYED FAIR EVEN WHEN NO ONE ELSE EXPECTED HIM TO! READ TO FIND OUT WHAT HAPPENED.

AS A YOUNG BOY, BOBBY JONES LIVED NEAR THE EAST LAKE COUNTRY CLUB IN ATLANTA. HE LOVED TO WATCH THE PROS PLAY GOLF.

HEY, KID! WHAT ARE YOU DOING?

LEARNING TO PLAY GOLF, MR. MAIDEN!

BY WATCHING ME? WELL, YOU'VE GOT A GOOD SWING GOING THERE!

THOUGH HE NEVER TOOK A LESSON, BOBBY BEGAN WINNING JUNIOR GOLF *TOURNAMENTS*.

THE WINNER OF THIS TOURNAMENT IS BOBBY JONES!

I CAN'T BELIEVE HE WON! HE'S ONLY SIX YEARS OLD!

STILL, BOBBY KEPT PLAYING, AND HE KEPT GETTING BETTER. HE WON HIS FIRST U.S. OPEN IN 1923. THEN, IN THE FINAL ROUND OF THE 1925 U.S. OPEN...

OH NO! THE BALL MOVED!

BOBBY WANTED TO WIN--BADLY--BUT HE DIDN'T HESITATE.

I WAS SETTING UP MY SHOT AND MY BALL MOVED SLIGHTLY. I'M CALLING A *PENALTY* ON MYSELF.

DID ANYONE SEE THE BALL MOVE?

NOPE, I DIDN'T SEE IT MOVE.

I DIDN'T EITHE[R]

BUT BOBBY INSISTED ON THE PENALTY.

JONES LOST THE TOURNAMENT BY JUST ONE STROKE! IF HE HADN'T CALLED THAT PENALTY...

NO ONE BUT HIM EVEN SAW HIS BALL MOVE! NOW THAT'S WHAT I CALL HONEST.

PEOPLE PRAISED BOBBY FOR WHAT HE'D DONE, BUT HE DIDN'T THINK THE PRAISE WAS NECESSARY.

THAT WAS THE MOST AMAZING DISPLAY OF SPORTSMANSHIP I'VE EVER SEEN!

YOU MAY AS WELL PRAISE A MAN FOR NOT ROBBING A BANK.*

* ACTUAL QUOTE

IN 1930, BOBBY JONES WON THE BRITISH AMATEUR, THE U.S. AMATEUR, THE BRITISH OPEN, AND THE U.S. OPEN. HE IS THE ONLY GOLFER TO EVER WIN ALL FOUR IN ONE YEAR.

TODAY, HE IS REMEMBERED AS ONE OF THE WORLD'S GREATEST ATHLETES, AS WELL AS A MODEL OF HONESTY AND SPORTSMANSHIP.

Bobby Jones completes "Grand Slam"

WHAT WOULD YOU DO?

YOU'RE PLAYING A BOARD GAME WITH A FRIEND. YOU'RE FRUSTRATED BECAUSE YOU'VE YET TO WIN.

"GUESS YOU'RE GOING TO LOSE AGAIN!" SAYS YOUR FRIEND. "AW, TOO BAD."

THE HOUSE PHONE RINGS AND YOUR FRIEND LEAVES THE ROOM. YOU HAVE A CHANCE TO MOVE A COUPLE OF PLAYING PIECES AND CHANGE THE GAME.

WHAT WOULD YOU DO?

MOHAMMED KHALIL

WHO IS HE?
A CAB DRIVER FROM NEWARK, NEW JERSEY

WHY HIM?
HE RETURNED SOMETHING OF GREAT VALUE TO ITS RIGHTFUL OWNER.

IT'S IMPORTANT TO BE HONEST, ESPECIALLY WHEN YOU'RE TEMPTED NOT TO BE. MOHAMMED KHALIL KNEW THAT. HE REMAINED HONEST IN A SITUATION THAT OTHER PEOPLE MIGHT HAVE TAKEN *ADVANTAGE* OF.

PHILIPPE QUINT IS A GRAMMY-NOMINATED VIOLINIST.

ONE NIGHT, PHILIPPE RETURNED HOME LATE FROM A CONCERT IN DALLAS.

IT'S AFTER MIDNIGHT. I'VE GOT TO FIND A TAXI.

HOW MUCH TO GET TO MANHATTAN?

ABOUT $50

THAT'S FINE. JUST PLEASE GET ME HOME AS FAST AS YOU CAN.

GOOD NIGHT, SIR.

WHAT? OH, THANKS. I MEAN, GOOD NIGHT.

OKAY. TIME TO GET TO BED.

WAIT A MINUTE...

OH NO!!! MY VIOLIN!! IT'S STILL IN THE BACK SEAT!

*ACTUAL QUOTE

TO SHOW HIS **GRATITUDE**, PHILIPPE GAVE A PRIVATE 30-MINUTE CONCERT IN A PARKING LOT NEAR THE NEWARK AIRPORT. ABOUT 100 CAB DRIVERS, INCLUDING MOHAMMED KHALIL, ATTENDED.

I'VE NEVER HEARD SUCH BEAUTIFUL MUSIC.

MOHAMMED ALSO RECEIVED A REWARD, AND THE MAYOR OF NEWARK PRESENTED HIM WITH A SPECIAL CITY **MEDALLION**.

THIS IS A MOMENT WHERE A CAB DRIVER IN OUR CITY SAW SOMETHING **AWRY** AND DID NOT TAKE PERSONAL ADVANTAGE, BUT DID THE RIGHT THING, SHOWED CHARACTER, SHOWED **ETHICS**, SHOWED VALUES, SHOWED A SENSE OF LOVE FOR HIS FELLOW MAN OR WOMAN.*

ACTUAL QUOTE

AS IT TURNS OUT, THAT WAS MOHAMMED'S LAST NIGHT ON THE JOB--HE WAS PLANNING TO RETIRE THE NEXT DAY! HE FELT GOOD THAT THE LAST THING HE DID WAS RETURN THE VIOLIN TO PHILIPPE QUINT.

MOHAMMED ACTED WITH GREAT HONESTY. HOW MANY PEOPLE WOULD HAVE DONE WHAT HE DID?

WHAT WOULD YOU DO?

YOU'RE IN A PARK, AND YOU SEE SOMEONE WALK OFF AND ACCIDENTALLY LEAVE HIS MP3 PLAYER BEHIND. YOU COULD CALL AFTER HIM, OR YOU COULD LET HIM KEEP WALKING AND MAYBE KEEP THE PLAYER FOR YOURSELF. AFTER ALL, WHO WOULD KNOW?

WHAT WOULD YOU DO IN THIS SITUATION?

ELLEN SZITA

WHO IS SHE?
A SINGLE MOTHER OF FOUR

WHY HER?
AT THE AGE OF 45, ELLEN TOLD THE TRUTH ABOUT NOT BEING ABLE TO READ OR WRITE.

SOMETIMES PEOPLE LIE IF THEY FEEL EMBARRASSED OR ASHAMED ABOUT SOMETHING. THAT'S HOW ELLEN SZITA FELT ABOUT BEING ILLITERATE— NOT BEING ABLE TO READ OR WRITE.

WHEN SHE FINALLY ADMITTED HER SECRET, ELLEN'S ENTIRE LIFE CHANGED. FIND OUT HOW.

ELLEN SZITA WAS BORN IN ENGLAND IN 1941. AS A CHILD, SHE WAS TAUGHT THAT SCHOOL WAS NOT IMPORTANT, ESPECIALLY FOR GIRLS.

YOUR JOB IS TO GET MARRIED AND TAKE CARE OF YOUR FAMILY, ELLEN. YOU DON'T NEED BOOKS FOR THAT.

HER MOTHER'S MESSAGE WASN'T REALLY NECESSARY.

YOU'RE IN THE "D" GROUP AGAIN, ELLEN. YOUR READING AND WRITING SKILLS ARE VERY POOR.

GREAT. D FOR DUNCE... I HATE SCHOOL.

ELLEN ALSO BECAME INVOLVED IN THE LITERACY MOVEMENT. SHE SITS ON SIX LITERACY BOARDS AND GIVES TALKS AT HIGH SCHOOLS, COLLEGES, AND UNIVERSITIES.

ILLITERACY BREEDS ILLITERACY...

IN 2009, READER'S DIGEST NAMED ELLEN ITS EDUCATION HERO. SHE HAS NEVER REGRETTED HER DECISION TO BE HONEST ABOUT HER ILLITERACY.

I MAY BE 60 YEARS OLD, BUT I FEEL AS THOUGH MY STORY HAS JUST BEGUN.*

*ACTUAL QUOTE

WHY DID ELLEN FINALLY DECIDE TO BE HONEST ABOUT HER PROBLEM? IT MIGHT HAVE BEEN BECAUSE SHE REALIZED THAT NOT BEING HONEST WAS HURTING HER FAMILY. SHE ALSO WANTED TO HELP HERSELF FEEL BETTER. IN TURN, SHE ENDED UP HELPING OTHERS.

DO YOU THINK BEING HONEST WITH YOURSELF IS IMPORTANT? LET'S FIND OUT.

WHAT WOULD YOU DO?

YOU'RE IN MATH CLASS LEARNING A TRICKY LESSON ABOUT FRACTIONS. THE TEACHER IS RUSHING THROUGH THE LESSON AND YOU AND SOME OTHER KIDS ARE LEFT FEELING CONFUSED.

"CAN WE MOVE ON?" YOUR TEACHER ASKS. "DOES EVERYONE UNDERSTAND THIS?"

YOU DON'T GET IT, BUT YOU DON'T WANT TO BE THE ONLY ONE TO SAY "NO."

WHAT WOULD YOU DO?

JEFFREY WIGAND

WHO IS HE?
FORMER LEAD RESEARCHER AT A LARGE AMERICAN TOBACCO COMPANY

WHY HIM?
HE TOLD THE TRUTH ABOUT THE DANGERS OF CIGARETTES.

SOMETIMES, LARGE COMPANIES WILL DO ANYTHING TO MAKE MONEY. THEY DON'T CARE THAT THEY MAY BE PUTTING OTHERS AT RISK.

JEFFREY WIGAND TOLD THE TOBACCO INDUSTRY'S DARKEST SECRETS ABOUT THE EFFECTS OF SMOKING. BUT BEING HONEST PUT HIM AND HIS FAMILY IN DANGER. FIND OUT WHAT HE DID.

JEFFREY WIGAND HAD ALWAYS LOVED SCIENCE AND MEDICINE. HE GOT HIS PHD IN **BIOCHEMISTRY** AND BEGAN WORKING AT HEALTH CARE COMPANIES.

WELCOME TO JOHNSON AND JOHNSON, DR. WIGAND.

GLAD TO BE HERE!

IN 1988, JEFFREY WENT TO WORK AT BROWN & WILLIAMSON, THE THIRD LARGEST TOBACCO COMPANY IN THE COUNTRY.

ONE PROJECT WE WANT YOU TO WORK ON IS THE DEVELOPMENT OF A NEW, HEALTHIER CIGARETTE.

SOME PEOPLE SMOKE, SO LET'S TRY AND MAKE IT SAFER.

AND THAT BIG NEW **SALARY** DOESN'T HURT EITHER, DOES IT, JEFFREY?

BUT AS HE CONTINUED TO WORK FOR THE COMPANY, JEFFREY MADE SOME SHOCKING DISCOVERIES.

WAIT A MINUTE. I WAS AT THIS MEETING. EVERYONE WAS TALKING ABOUT HOW CIGARETTES CAUSE CANCER AND HEART DISEASE. BUT THE REPORT DOESN'T MENTION ANY OF THAT!

JEFFREY LEARNED OTHER UPSETTING THINGS, TOO. HE FINALLY DECIDED TO TALK TO THE COMPANY CEO, THOMAS SANDEFUR.

WE PUT THINGS IN OUR CIGARETTES TO HOOK PEOPLE ON SMOKING. AND OUR PIPE TOBACCO CAUSES *TUMORS!* IT HAS TO STOP.

CHANGES LIKE THAT WOULD BE BAD FOR BUSINESS, WIGAND.

BUT...

YOUR "SAFE CIGARETTE" PROJECT IS OVER, TOO. IT WOULD DRAW ATTENTION TO PROBLEMS IN OUR OTHER PRODUCTS.

IN 1993, BROWN & WILLIAMSON DECIDED JEFFREY WAS TOO BIG A RISK TO KEEP ON.

WE DIDN'T FIRE HIM A MINUTE TOO SOON. THIS GUY IS TROUBLE.

GIVE ME THOSE NOTES! AND THAT JOURNAL IS MINE!

SOON AFTER JEFFREY WAS FIRED, A LAW FIRM CONTACTED HIM.

GIVE THEM TO ME.

WE WANT TO SUE THE BIG TOBACCO COMPANIES, DR. WIGAND. BUT WE NEED YOUR HELP TO UNDERSTAND THESE REPORTS.

19

NOT LONG AFTER THAT...

IT'S FROM BROWN AND WILLIAMSON. THEY'RE **SUSPENDING** OUR HEALTH INSURANCE. THEY MUST HAVE FOUND OUT THAT I'M HELPING THAT LAW FIRM.

JEFFREY DIDN'T BACK DOWN. LATER, HE WAS APPROACHED BY **60** MINUTES, A NEWS SHOW THAT INVESTIGATES IMPORTANT STORIES.

WE WANT AN INSIDER'S VIEW ON WHAT GOES ON IN THE TOBACCO INDUSTRY.

I'LL TELL YOU WHAT I KNOW, MR. WALLACE.

JEFFREY WENT ON THE SHOW AND TOLD THE TRUTH ABOUT BROWN & WILLIAMSON.

...SO BROWN & WILLIAMSON'S EXECUTIVES KNEW ALL ALONG THAT NICOTINE IS ADDICTIVE AND THAT THEIR TOBACCO PRODUCTS CAUSE CANCER.

YES, THAT'S RIGHT. BUT WE'RE IN A NICOTINE DELIVERY BUSINESS. YOU'LL GET YOUR FIX.*

BEFORE THE INTERVIEW AIRED, SOME OF THE DETAILS LEAKED OUT AND COST BROWN & WILLIAMSON MILLIONS OF DOLLARS. THE COMPANY SUED JEFFREY. THEN THINGS GOT EVEN WORSE.

SOMEONE LEFT A BULLET IN MY MAILBOX. WELL. IF B & W IS TRYING SCARE **TACTICS**, THEY'VE PICKED THE WRONG PERSON.

20

*ACTUAL QUOTE

EVENTUALLY, THE *60 MINUTES* SEGMENT WAS AIRED. LATER, IN A HUGE COURT CASE, JEFFREY GAVE IMPORTANT *TESTIMONY* THAT HELPED WIN A $368 BILLION SETTLEMENT FROM THE TOBACCO INDUSTRY.

WOW! THAT'S A HUGE AMOUNT!

IT'S THE AMOUNT THE STATES HAD SPENT TO TREAT THE DISEASES CAUSED BY SMOKING.

[TO]DAY, JEFFREY WIGAND CONTINUES TO SPEAK [O]UT AGAINST TOBACCO. HE HAS ALSO CREATED [A] NON-PROFIT ORGANIZATION, CALLED SMOKE-[FR]EE KIDS, TO HELP REDUCE TEEN SMOKING.

MAKE SMART DECISIONS. AND IF YOU'VE STARTED SMOKING—STOP.

WOW! IT'S ONE THING TO BE HONEST. IT'S ANOTHER THING TO BE HONEST WHEN IT CAN GET YOU IN TROUBLE! BUT JEFFREY WIGAND TOOK THE RISK. HE STILL TALKS ABOUT "FEELING COMPELLED TO SPEAK THE TRUTH."

NOW LET'S SEE HOW YOU'D HANDLE A DIFFICULT SITUATION.

WHAT WOULD YOU DO?

YOU SEE SOME KIDS FROM YOUR NEIGHBORHOOD SHOPLIFTING IN A STORE. ONE OF THEM LOOKS UP AND SEES YOU WATCHING THEM.

YOU KNOW WHAT THEY'RE DOING IS WRONG. BUT IF YOU TELL SECURITY, THOSE KIDS WILL PROBABLY GUESS WHO REPORTED THEM.

WHAT DO YOU DO?

21

PHYLLIS PENZO

ROBERT CUNNINGHAM

WHO ARE THEY?
A NEW YORK CITY WAITRESS AND A NEW YORK CITY POLICE DETECTIVE

WHY THEM?
A SHARED LOTTERY TICKET TAUGHT THEM WHAT HONESTY REALLY MEANS.

SOME PEOPLE AREN'T HONEST UNLESS THEY HAVE TO BE. ROBERT CUNNINGHAM ISN'T ONE OF THOSE PEOPLE. LET'S SEE HOW HIS GOOD **FORTUNE**--AND HIS HONESTY--CHANGED TWO LIVES.

PHYLLIS PENZO ENJOYED BEING A WAITRESS AT SAL'S PIZZERIA. SOMETIMES, THOUGH...

I CAN IMAGINE! THIS IS YOUR SIXTH DAY IN A ROW. AND LONG SHIFTS EACH TIME!

I FEEL LIKE I'M BEING RUN OFF MY FEET TODAY!

ROBERT CUNNINGHAM, A POLICE DETECTIVE, WAS A REGULAR CUSTOMER AT SAL'S.

I WONDER WHERE BOB IS TONIGHT. HE'S USUALLY HERE BY EIGHT O'CLOCK, RIGHT AFTER HIS SHIFT. HIS LINGUINI AND CLAM SAUCE IS ALL READY FOR HIM!

HEY, AL! HI, JANE.

AND PHYLLIS! HOW'S MY FAVORITE WAITRESS?

AT THE DINER THE NEXT NIGHT, PHYLLIS WAS BUSY WHEN BOB SHOWED UP. SHE HADN'T EVEN LISTENED FOR THE NUMBERS THE NIGHT BEFORE.

YOUR LINGUINI WILL BE UP IN A MINUTE, BOB.

HOLD ON A MINUTE, PHYL. I HAVE TO TELL YOU SOMETHING IMPORTANT...

WHAT?

WE WON $6 MILLION! 3 MILLION EACH!

I CAN'T TAKE ANY MONEY, BOB. YOU BOUGHT THE TICKET. AND IF YOU HADN'T TOLD ME, I WOULDN'T HAVE KNOWN!

YEAH, BUT I WOULD HAVE. BESIDES, YOU DID PICK THREE OF THE NUMBERS!

ROBERT NEVER EVEN CONSIDERED KEEPING ALL THE MONEY FOR HIMSELF. HE PROVED THAT OLD-FASHIONED HONESTY STILL EXISTS!

I'VE BEEN A SIMPLE PERSON ALL MY LIFE. IF I SAY I'LL DO SOMETHING, I DO IT.*

*ACTUAL QUOTE

24

PHYLLIS TRAVELED AND BOUGHT A HOUSE WITH HER WINNINGS. SHE ALSO GAVE HER DAUGHTER A BIG PRESENT

WOW, MOM! I DON'T KNOW WHAT TO SAY!!

ROBERT BOUGHT A BOAT AND ADDED ON TO HIS HOUSE.

NO ONE WOULD HAVE EXPECTED ROBERT CUNNINGHAM TO ACTUALLY SPLIT THE $6 MILLION WITH PHYLLIS, BUT HE DIDN'T EVEN THINK TWICE ABOUT IT! HE DIDN'T LET THE MONEY AFFECT HIS VALUES OR HIS HONESTY.

NOW WE'LL HAVE THE HOUSE WE'VE ALWAYS DREAMED OF! WHAT ELSE CAN WE ASK FOR?

WHAT WOULD YOU DO?

YOUR PARENTS GIVE YOU MONEY SO YOU AND YOUR BROTHER CAN BUY NEW SHOES. THEY TELL YOU TO SPLIT IT EQUALLY SO BOTH YOU AND YOUR BROTHER CAN GET THE SHOES YOU LIKE.

YOUR MOM GIVES YOU THE MONEY WHILE YOUR BROTHER IS OUTSIDE PLAYING. HE WON'T KNOW HOW MUCH YOU HAVE. YOU COULD BUY THE SHOES YOU WANT AND KEEP A LITTLE EXTRA TO GO TO THE MOVIES LATER!

WHAT WOULD YOU DO?

BEING HONEST ABOUT MONEY

KELLI OWENS

WHO IS SHE?
A YOUNG SINGLE MOTHER OF THREE

WHY HER?
SHE WAS HONEST IN A VERY TEMPTING SITUATION.

IT'S IMPORTANT TO BE HONEST WHEN YOU FIND SOMETHING THAT DOESN'T BELONG TO YOU. BUT WHAT IF NOT BEING HONEST COULD MAKE A BIG DIFFERENCE IN YOUR LIFE? KELLI OWENS HAD TO ASK HERSELF THAT QUESTION. LET'S SEE WHAT SHE DECIDED.

KELLI OWENS, A SINGLE MOTHER OF THREE KIDS, WAS FACING SOME HARD TIMES. THERE JUST WASN'T ENOUGH MONEY TO SUPPORT HER CHILDREN.

MOMMY, DO WE HAVE ENOUGH MONEY TO RIDE THE BUS?

MOMMY, UP, UP! PICK UP!

KELLI WORRIED ABOUT HOW SHE WAS GOING TO KEEP THE MONEY COMING IN...

I NEED TO LEARN SOME SKILLS. I HEARD THAT GOODWILL TRAINS PEOPLE AND EVEN GETS THEM JOBS. MAYBE THEY CAN HELP ME.

O ONE CLAIMED THE MONEY. BUT KELLI HAD *IMPRESSED* A LOT OF PEOPLE, INCLUDING *OODWILL* EXECUTIVE DIRECTOR BILL WYLIE.

THERE HAS TO BE A GREAT DEAL OF VALUE IN THAT PERSON'S SOUL TO...SAY THAT THE RIGHT THING TO DO IS TURN THIS IN.* SO THIS MONEY WILL NOW BE PUT INTO A *SCHOLARSHIP* FUND TO HELP KELLI WITH HER EDUCATION.

KELLI DID GO BACK TO SCHOOL. SHE PLANS TO HAVE A CAREER IN LAW *ENFORCEMENT*.

WHO WOULD HAVE THOUGHT THAT LIFE COULD CHANGE LIKE THIS? AND ALL FROM DOING THE RIGHT THING.

NOT MANY PEOPLE WOULD HAVE DONE WHAT KELLI DID. THAT MONEY COULD HAVE MADE A BIG DIFFERENCE IN HER LIFE. BUT SHE TURNED THE MONEY OVER WITHOUT HESITATION. NOW THAT'S HONESTY!

COULD YOU BE AS HONEST AS KELLI WAS?

WHAT WOULD YOU DO?

YOU AND YOUR FRIEND FIND A WALLET AT THE MALL. IT HAS NEARLY $200 AND SOME CREDIT CARDS IN IT.

"WE NEED TO TURN THIS IN," YOU SAY.

"NOT SO FAST," SAYS YOUR FRIEND. "WHAT IF WE TAKE SOME OF THE MONEY AS A KIND OF REWARD? THEN WE CAN DROP THE WALLET OFF AT THE SECURITY DESK. NO ONE WOULD EVER KNOW."

WHAT WOULD YOU DO?

*ACTUAL QUOTE

29

WEB SITES

VISIT THIS WEB SITE TO LEARN MORE ABOUT THE READ SOCIETY AND THE ORGANIZATION'S LEARNING PROGRAMS.

www.readsociety.bc.ca

VISIT THIS WEB SITE TO LEARN MORE ABOUT SMOKE-FREE KIDS, THE NON-PROFIT ORGANIZATION CREATED BY DR. JEFFREY WIGAND.

www.jeffreywigand.com/smokefreekids.php

READ MORE ABOUT BOBBY JONES' ACHIEVEMENTS AT THIS WEB SITE FOR THE WORLD GOLF HALL OF FAME.

www.wgv.com/hof/member.phpmember=1070

READ AN ESSAY ABOUT ILLITERACY BY ELLEN SZITA AT THIS WEB SITE.

www.writersblock.ca/spring2001/essay4.htm

GLOSSARY

ADVANTAGE SOMETHING THAT HELPS ONE BE IN A BETTER POSITION OR SITUATION

AMATEUR A PERSON WHO TAKES PART IN AN ACTIVITY WITHOUT BEING PAID

AWRY OFF THE RIGHT COURSE

BIOCHEMISTRY CHEMISTRY THAT DEALS WITH THE PROCESSES OCCURRING IN LIVING THINGS

ENFORCEMENT TO CARRY OUT EFFECTIVELY

ETHICS RULES ABOUT THE RIGHT AND WRONG WAY TO ACT

FACTORY A BUILDING CONTAINING MANUFACTURING EQUIPMENT

FORTUNE POSITIVE RESULTS THAT COME PARTLY BY CHANCE

GRATITUDE THE STATE OF FEELING GRATEFUL OR APPRECIATIVE

IMPRESSED TO BE AFFECTED STRONGLY OR DEEPLY

MEDALLION A LARGE MEDAL

PENALTY A PUNISHMENT GIVEN FOR BREAKING A RULE IN A SPORT OR GAME

SALARY MONEY PAID AT REGULAR TIMES FOR WORK

SCHOLARSHIP MONEY GIVEN TO A STUDENT TO HELP PAY FOR EDUCATION

SUSPENDING PUTTING SOMETHING ON HOLD OR STOPPING IT ALTOGETHER

TACTICS PLANNED ACTIONS FOR A PARTICULAR PURPOSE

TESTIMONY A STATEMENT MADE BY A WITNESS UNDER OATH, ESPECIALLY IN A COURT

TOURNAMENTS CONTESTS PLAYED FOR A CHAMPIONSHIP

TUMORS ABNORMAL MASSES OF TISSUE CELLS IN THE BODY

WISELY HAVING OR SHOWING GOOD SENSE OR JUDGMENT

INDEX

ASHAMED 14, 15

ATHLETE 9

ATLANTA 6

BROWN & WILLIAMSON 18, 19, 20

CIGARETTES 18, 19

CONCERT 10, 13

CUNNINGHAM, ROBERT 5, 22-25

DALLAS 10

DISEASE 19, 21

EDUCATION 17, 29

EMBARRASSED 14

ETHICS 13

FACTORY 15

FAMILY 14, 17, 18

GOLF 6-9

GRATITUDE 13

ILLITERACY 14, 16, 17

JONES, BOBBY 4, 6-9

KHALIL, MOHAMMED 4, 10-13

LOTTERY 22, 23

OWENS, KELLI 5, 26-29

PENALTY 8, 9

PENZO, PHYLLIS 5, 22-25

QUINT, PHILIPPE 10, 13

SECRET 14, 15, 18

SMOKE-FREE KIDS 21

SZITA, ELLEN 5, 14-17

TAXI 10, 12

TEMPER 7

TOBACCO INDUSTRY 18, 20, 21

VIOLIN 11, 12, 13

WIGAND, JEFFREY 5, 18-21